Mother Teresa

Published in the United States of America by Cherry Lake Publishing
Ann Arbor, Michigan
www.cherrylakepublishing.com

Content Adviser: Ryan Emery Hughes, Doctoral Student, School of Education, University of Michigan
Reading Adviser: Marla Conn MS, Ed., Literacy specialist, Read-Ability, Inc.
Book Design: Jennifer Wahi
Illustrator: Jeff Bane

Photo Credits: ©PjeterPeter/Wikimedia, 5; © Vittoriano Rastelli / Contributor/Getty, 7, 9; © Zvonimir Atletic/
Shutterstock, 11; © Sean Sprague / Alamy Stock Photo, 13, 22; © Tim Graham / Alamy Stock Photo, 15; © Dinodia
Photos / Alamy Stock Photo, 17; © Bettmann / Contributor/Getty, 19, 23; © TIM GRAHAM / Alamy Stock Photo,
21; Cover, 6, 14, 18, Jeff Bane; Various frames throughout, Shutterstock Images

Library of Congress Cataloging-in-Publication Data

Names: Haldy, Emma E., author.
Title: Mother Teresa / Emma E. Haldy.
Description: Ann Arbor, Michigan : Cherry Lake Publishing, 2017. | Series: My
    itty-bitty bio | Includes bibliographical references and index. |
    Audience: Grades K-3.
Identifiers: LCCN 2016031791| ISBN 9781634721547 (hardcover) | ISBN
    9781634722865 (pbk.) | ISBN 9781634722209 (pdf) | ISBN 9781634723527
    (ebook)
Subjects: LCSH: Teresa, Mother, Saint, 1910-1997--Juvenile literature |
    Missionaries of Charity--Biography--Juvenile literature. | Christian
    saints--India--Kolkata--Biography--Juvenile literature.
Classification: LCC BX4700.T397 H35 2017 | DDC 271/.97 [B] --dc23
LC record available at https://lccn.loc.gov/2016031791

Printed in the United States of America
Corporate Graphics

table of contents

About the author: Emma E. Haldy is a former librarian and a proud Michigander. She lives with her husband, Joe, and an ever-growing collection of books.

About the illustrator: Jeff Bane and his two business partners own a studio along the American River in Folsom, California, home of the 1849 Gold Rush. When Jeff's not sketching or illustrating for clients, he's either swimming or kayaking in the river to relax.

I was born in 1910. I lived in the country of Macedonia.

My family was **Catholic**.

I loved my mother. She was kind. She was **generous**.

She taught me about **charity**.

I wanted to focus on my faith.
I became a **nun**.

I was sent to the country of India.
I taught in a school.

What do you want to do when you grow up?

I was good at my job. I helped poor students.

I tried to give them a better life.

But I wanted to do more. I felt a calling.

I wanted to help the poorest of the poor.

I moved to the **slums**.

I opened a school. I opened a **shelter** for the dying.

I fed the hungry. I cared for the ill. I comforted the lonely.

I **inspired** others to help.
More nuns joined me.

We devoted our lives to helping the poor.

How do you think you
can help others?

The world honored my work.
I won many awards.

I kept working. I wanted to help more people.

I died at the age of 87. In 2016, I became a Catholic saint.

I was a **compassionate** woman. I believed in peace. I spread love.

What would you like to ask me?

1948

1910

Born
1910

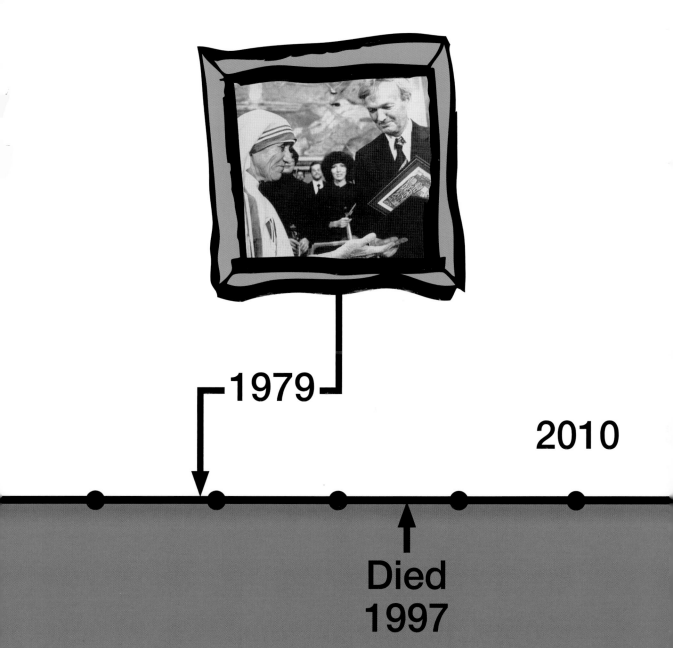

1979

2010

Died
1997

glossary

charity (CHAR-ih-tee) kindness toward others

Catholic (KATH-uh-lik) a member of the Roman Catholic church

compassionate (kuhm-PASH-uhn-it) feeling a desire to help someone who is suffering

generous (JEN-ur-uhs) willing and happy to give to and share with others

inspired (in-SPYRD) to fill someone with the interest and strength to do something

nun (NUHN) a woman who lives in a religious community of women and has devoted her life to her religion

shelter (SHEL-tur) a place where someone without a home can stay

slums (SLUHMZ) overcrowded areas in cities where poor people live

index